When a child asks to take communion

Daphne Kirk

kevin mayhew

First published in 2003 by
KEVIN MAYHEW LTD
Buxhall, Stowmarket, Suffolk, IP14 3BW
E-mail: info@kevinmayhewltd.com

KINGSGATE PUBLISHING INC
1000 Pannell Street, Suite G, Columbia, MO 65201
E-mail: sales@kingsgatepublishing.com

© 2003 Daphne Kirk

The right of Daphne Kirk to be identified as the author of this work has been asserted by her in accordance with the Copyright, Designs and Patents Act 1988.

No part of this publication may be reproduced, stored in a retrieval system, or transmitted, in any form or by any means, electronic, mechanical, photocopying, recording or otherwise, without the prior written permission of the publisher. All rights reserved.

Except where indicated, Scripture quotations are taken from the Holy Bible, New International Version. Copyright © 1973, 1978, 1984 by International Bible Society. Used by permission of Hodder & Stoughton Limited. All rights reserved.

9 8 7 6 5 4 3 2 1 0

ISBN 1 84417 056 X
Catalogue No 1500580

Cover design by Angela Selfe
Edited by Katherine Laidler
Typeset by Richard Weaver
Printed and bound in Great Britain

Contents

	Introduction	5
CHAPTER 1	Exploring communion	7
CHAPTER 2	The vision, system and method	13
CHAPTER 3	The practice today	15
CHAPTER 4	What do we tell the children?	19
CHAPTER 5	Celebrating communion today	21
CHAPTER 6	Our love song!	27
	Other books by Daphne Kirk	32

To Joy, my daughter and friend.
Thank you for encouraging and challenging me,
for praying and holding on to the vision.
Your faithfulness has been an inspiration to me.

Introduction

- When a child asks to take communion what will you say?
- As parents do you wonder what to do with children when it comes to communion?
- As parents do you wonder how to explain communion to your children?
- Are you in church leadership and facing making policies in respect of communion?
- Have you considered the biblical perspective and history of communion?
- Have you considered how we can celebrate communion more like the early Church?

I hope this book will give you wisdom, taking you directly to the Word of God as this celebration is unfolded, that you will be as inspired and excited as I have been writing it and that the rich treasure of the Word will come alive and lead to a transformation of your homes and communities.

God is calling children and young people from the nations, a mighty army rising to take the gospel to the ends of the earth, and he has commissioned us to raise them for 'such a time as this'! Let's raise them according to the heart of the Father and in his way.

Chapter 1

Exploring communion

The journey

Where did the journey begin that has led us to the time we call communion, or the Lord's Supper, and does that journey tell us anything about the involvement of children?

Exodus tells of the first time the people of Israel (adults, young people and children) celebrated Passover. God commanded that the Israelites (adults, young people and children) remembered and celebrated annually the deliverance of their firstborn sons from death by the shedding of the blood of an unblemished lamb, and their subsequent release from Egypt, the land of their bondage. On the tenth day of the first month each man was to take a lamb for his family, one for each household. If any of the households were too small for one lamb, then they were to share one with their nearest neighbour (Exodus 12:4).

On the fourteenth day the lamb was to be slaughtered at twilight and the blood put on the sides and tops of the doorframes of the houses where they (adults, young people and children) were going to eat the lamb, as they stood dressed and ready to leave Egypt. The blood of the lamb would be a sign, so when the Lord saw the blood he would pass over their home and the firstborn would live and not die.

This celebration took place in households; every age group was involved. It was an interactive time where the children heard the story of God's deliverance of the people from Egypt and how the Lord saw the blood and passed over their homes so they could live. They could ask questions: 'When your children ask you, "What does this ceremony mean to you?" tell them, "It is the Passover sacrifice to the Lord who passed over the houses of the Israelites in Egypt and spared our homes when he struck down the Israelites"' (Exodus 13:14).

And so the people were commanded that 'This day is a day you are to commemorate; for the generations to come you shall celebrate it as a festival to the Lord.' That celebration continued so that Jesus kept the Passover from childhood, until the day came when he celebrated it for the last time with his disciples.

After Jesus' death and resurrection we read in Acts 2 that Peter addressed the crowd: 'Fellow Jews and all of you who live in Jerusalem (adults, young people and children) . . . repent and be baptised, every one of you (adults, young people and children) in the name of Christ Jesus for the forgiveness of your sins. And you will receive the gift of the Holy Spirit. The promise is for you and your children and all who are far off – for all whom the Lord will call . . . Those who accepted his message were baptised and about three thousand were added to the number that day. They devoted themselves to the apostles' teaching and to the fellowship, to the breaking of bread and to prayer. Everyone (adults, young people and children) was filled with awe . . . They broke bread in their homes and ate together with glad and sincere hearts' (Acts 2:38, 41-43a, 46b).

Communion was an event that was birthed in the home at the time of the Passover, to celebrate and remember that the mighty hand of God had delivered them. When the early Church was birthed, in the Acts of the Apostles, the Passover was still being celebrated in homes. The story of deliverance was still being told. At Passover it was the story of deliverance from Egypt as the Lord saw the blood; in Acts it was the story of deliverance from the kingdom of darkness through the shed blood of the risen Lamb of God.

Just as Passover was a time where children were told the story and encouraged to ask questions, the same opportunity remained in the informal atmosphere of the homes of the believers in the early Church. There children heard the story of redemption and their parents recounting their own salvation through the power of the blood of the Lamb, as they broke bread from house to house, with 'glad and sincere hearts'.

Children were part of the celebration of the greatest victory in the history of humanity.

The sacrifice

In the Old Testament when the sacrifice was laid on the altar it was a time of personal repentance and a very serious occasion where sins were forgiven. The fat was burned as a food offering to the Lord (Leviticus 3:11, 16-17), the priest had his share (Leviticus 7:14), and the rest was taken home for the family where a household festival was held and friends were invited (Leviticus 7:12).

When Jesus offered himself on the cross this became the place for our personal repentance and reconciliation with God. Jesus became the sacrifice so that 'whosoever' (every adult, young person and child) came to that altar could walk away free, reconciled to God and each other (John 3:16). The agony of our sin was put on Jesus and he became the ultimate sacrifice that gave us our freedom today.

The cross is still the place for personal repentance and a solemn moment for the forgiveness of our sin. Here we experience God's love as we confess our sin, repent and receive forgiveness. The lamb became the Lamb who was sacrificed on the altar of the cross. This time there was no need for further sacrifices. Sin was defeated for ever! At the cross there is repentance but also total victory. Just as the Old Testament sacrifice was then taken for a household celebration of freedom, so Jesus gave us his body and blood in the bread and wine to celebrate our redemption.

The meal

The disciples sat around a Passover meal table with the Lord. It was a time of communal sharing of food and fellowship, just as the Jews had experienced under the old covenant meal for centuries. On that very night all over Israel the Jewish people would have been sharing together around the Passover meal.

The disciples did not know that this Passover meal was to be very different, not in outward appearance but right at the heart of what they were experiencing. Jesus was the host, and in an atmosphere of thanks he broke the bread saying that it was his body (the sacrifice laid on the altar). After they had finished the supper he poured out the wine as his own blood (shed at the altar). The disciples discovered that at this Passover meal the Lamb himself was hosting the meal, looking to his own death and at the same time looking to the day of great rejoicing when he would drink the cup again with them in his Father's Kingdom (Luke 22).

Around this meal table he gave the command: 'Do this in remembrance of me.'

The celebration

The Jewish people enjoyed celebrating together. They had national festivals such as Hezekiah's celebration: 'When the offerings were finished . . . they sang praises with gladness and bowed their heads and worshipped.' After the Passover offerings had been made they had a two-week celebration for the whole nation and 'there was great joy in Jerusalem . . . and God heard them, for their prayer reached heaven, His holy dwelling-place' (2 Chronicles 29 and 30). The people (adults, young people and children) had the greatest party since the days of Solomon!

Jesus used the Jewish custom of the Passover celebration in which to be remembered. He chose this as a time to look forward also to the great celebration that would take place as a banquet in heaven, saying that he would not take part in this again until the marriage supper of the Lamb (Revelation 19). Jesus was looking forward to a time of great rejoicing, a time of reunion! Although as he broke bread he was on a journey to his own agonising death, he looked past that to his return to his Father when his redeemed ones (adults, young people and children) would join in the greatest celebration of all times at the wedding feast of the Lamb.

This continued with the early Church celebrating with great enthusiasm 'in their homes with glad and sincere hearts'. It remained a thanksgiving meal. They had their life, and worship centred on the breaking of bread in a meal that was a joyful expression of deliverance and in honour of their risen Lord (Acts 2:46). For the early Church the home was the church building, as seen in Romans 16:23 when 'the whole church met in the home of Gaius'.

Three thousand gathered in homes around the Word with praise and prayer (Acts 2). They could not celebrate enough: they celebrated daily. Could it be that as 2000 years have passed, so has the joy and celebration of the resurrection life and that we have lost the excitement of looking forward to sharing together at the wedding supper of the Lamb? Three thousand invaded the homes and celebrated!

Is our celebration of communion still in such an atmosphere of joyous celebration?

The experience to be remembered

Passover was a family meal (Deuteronomy 12:7) when families ate and celebrated together in the presence of the Lord. They were told to continue to celebrate the Passover as a lasting memorial to their descendants and to the generations to come. It was to be a part of their culture so that their children, their children's children and all their descendants would continue to rejoice and remember. This command, given by God, was so effective that still today the Jewish people celebrate, and their children participate and remember!

In Acts 2:46 communion was an interactive meal for the whole community which ate in a joyful celebration. The sacrificed was remembered in the context of the freedom they now enjoyed. How the children must have loved these occasions and looked forward to them, as they had an experience with the Word in the context of their friends and small community of believers. This was the Word and experience, in perfect harmony with one another and the most powerful way for children, or adults, to learn and to have the message of the cross forever imprinted on their lives. None of us truly understands the fullness of the covenant we celebrate – we are all on a journey of understanding – but, in the atmosphere of informality and relationship within the home, a continual life-changing experience can be forever engraved on the hearts of those present, including the children.

The lifestyle to be honoured

Paul wrote to the Corinthian church because as a community they were not showing the life of those who had truly been transformed by the cross (1 Corinthians 11:17-22). Their meal was held according to social status and in an atmosphere of disorderliness. Their attitudes and resulting behaviour meant that 'they drank judgement on themselves'. The meal was being held in honour of Jesus but everything about it was contrary to the sacrifice that they were celebrating.

Calvary had removed social, racial, gender, generational and every form of division, and so should have resulted in a meal that expressed the prayer of Jesus in John 17:21, 'that all of them may be one': a meal of total unity.

When Paul talked about discerning the body he was referring to the Body of Jesus: that Body was now the living expression of him around the meal table. Jesus was the Incarnate One manifest in his new Body, the Church (adults, young people and children) living daily in each other's presence in their homes in unity, totally sensitive to the Incarnate One. They were to be the sacred Body with Christ dwelling in them. People would look and say, 'God is really among you!' (1 Corinthians 11:24-25).

We are still to be the community manifesting Jesus, his new Body, his living testimony to the power of his sacrifice and an expression of the joy of that freedom and reconciliation. The meal is an outward expression of that commitment to Jesus and to each other resulting from the transformation in each life (1 Corinthians 10.18).

At the cross we came to personal repentance; at the meal table we are to come to a corporate expression of unity. All divisions are to be reconciled, all differences laid down to show the life of the Kingdom in total harmony, unity and 'in one accord'. At this time of celebration the emphasis is on corporate unity and bringing down of divisions; personal repentance was for the cross, or the altar where the lamb was offered.

Chapter 2

The vision, system and method

Vision: what did God want to achieve?

Pharaoh refused to let the people of Israel go and God told Moses to tell Pharaoh, 'By now I could have stretched out my hand and struck you and your people with a plague that would have wiped you off the earth. But I have raised you up for this very purpose, that I might show you my power and that my name might be proclaimed in all the earth' (Exodus 9:15-16).

Here was God's vision: 'That my name might be proclaimed in all the earth.'

System: how was God going to ensure that this would continue?

In Exodus 10:1-2 God said to Moses, 'Go to Pharaoh for I have hardened his heart and the hearts of the officials so that I may perform these miraculous signs of mine among them.' And here is the system: 'that you may tell your children and grandchildren how I dealt harshly with the Egyptians and how I performed my signs among them, and that you may know that I am Lord.'

The system that God would use to spread his name was by the Israelites passing on these stories to their children and grandchildren through the generations. And that they were 'to commemorate for the generations to come'. The name of God was to be passed down the generations as one generation told the next in a feast celebrated in their homes.

Method: what were the people to do?

In Exodus 12 the Israelites were told how to celebrate Passover. This festival would be the method they used to ensure that they and their children always remembered what their God had done in sparing their lives and delivering them from Egypt. So important was it that God even gave specific space for the children to interact and ensure they fully understood what their God had done as they ate this meal together.

Vision affirmed: what does God still want to achieve?

Jesus affirmed the vision when he gave the Great Commission. His call was to make disciples of all nations, that his name might be declared in all the earth (Matthew 28:18-20).

System retained: how will he ensure that this will continue?

The command to pass on the story to our children and the next generation has never been revoked; it is God's perfect way of ensuring that his salvation be established from generation to generation.

Method exploded: what are we to do?

As the early Church broke bread from house to house daily, not annually as the Passover, every day more people joined them (Acts 2:42-47). The method was going to the ends of the earth, even to the Gentiles.

Today we celebrate the freedom and life that is a direct result of the cross. Just as in the Old Testament people celebrated after the sacrifice, so we today can celebrate having been to the cross and received the forgiveness and new life so freely given to us there.

Chapter 3
The practice today

How can we begin to enter communion with Jesus and with each other in the way that Jesus showed us and in the way that the early dynamic Church continued the practice? If you are a pastor or senior leader of your church this book will give you a forum to talk and share together from the foundations of the Word, and to reappraise your own vision for this time. It may cause you to consider:

- What are your policies in relation to children and communion?
- What place and expression does communion have in our larger celebrations?
- What place and expression does it have in our small groups and our homes?

For those of you who are parents or heads of your own households, I would encourage you to restore communion to your homes. Reinstate it and bring it back to life.

What are the key elements of the meal that we can see taken from the Passover (Exodus 12), Jesus' last supper with his disciples (Matthew 26) and the early Church (Acts 2)?

- The Passover meal belonged to the Lord.
  And communion still does!
- Breaking of bread was an ongoing, eventually daily, celebration in homes.
  And still can be!
- Passover was a festival, a time to rejoice and be glad. The early Church celebrated communion with great joy.
  We can celebrate in this way too!
- The meal was about passing on a personal testimony of deliverance by the mighty hand of God, never to be forgotten.
  And still is!

- The bread and the wine were central: the body and the blood of the sacrificed lamb (Lamb).
  And still are!
- In the Old Testament, Passover was a time to celebrate freedom and deliverance from bondage and to look forward to the time they would enter their land of freedom in the Promised Land. Jesus celebrated deliverance by his own death and looked forward to the celebration in his Father's house where the meal and festival would continue.
  We can still do this!
- The Passover and the breaking of bread in the early Church were in the environment of signs and wonders.
  Let's pray for their return!
- The meal was taken in a spirit of unity, sincerity, thankfulness and awe.
  And still can be!
- The atmosphere was one of a mealtime interaction with questions and answers included.
  And still can be!
- There was food and drink at a meal where the bread was to be eaten and the wine to be drunk.
  And still can be!
- Passover and communion were celebrations taking place in homes where the children were a very natural part.
  And still can be!
- They were a shared experience.
  And still can be!
- Communion was a living testimony of people expressing the Good News shown in their lives together.
  And still can be!
- Passover was about a personal testimony and explanation: 'On that day tell your sons I do this because of what the Lord did for me when he bought me out of bondage' (Exodus 13:8).
  And communion still is!

- The conversation around the meal table was about the Lamb (the risen Lord) and the impact that he has had on their lives together, in the promised land of deliverance because of the sacrifice.
  And still can be!
- Passover and communion were reminders for those taking part and for the generations to come.
  And still are!

These elements should still be the focus, the environment, the atmosphere and the reason to celebrate today. We celebrate our risen Lamb who has redeemed us and our children from the slavery of sin and bought us, and our children, into the Kingdom of the resurrected Lamb of God who is preparing the wedding feast for us in the house of his Father. There this wonderful celebration will have its final fulfilment (Luke 22:16).

Chapter 4

What do we tell the children?

Children understand most by the interactive way we communicate and also by the heart attitude that we express in relationship with them.

What do we need to tell them? The following points will give some guidelines:

- Tell them about how in the Old Testament people had to bring a lamb to be killed so their sins could be taken away as the lamb's blood was shed. Then tell them how they took the meat and had a celebration meal because they were free of their sin.

- Tell them the story of deliverance from Egypt and how the people celebrated the Passover meal. Communicate the greatness of God in setting the Israelites free and saving their firstborn sons when they put the blood of the lamb on their homes. Tell them how much he loved the Israelites and how grateful they would have been to be able to go to their own country and live without slavery. They celebrated Passover so they would never forget what God had done for them and so their children would know.

- Tell them about the Passover supper that Jesus had with his disciples. That he was telling them about his death, and how he would shed his blood like the lamb in the Old Testament so no more sacrifices would have to be made for our sin, and also about the wonderful feast we will have with him one day in heaven. Communicate how much he loved them and that he wanted us to remember that love through this special meal.

- Tell them about the Cross and how we can have our sin forgiven because Jesus died there and his blood makes it possible for us to repent (say we are really, really sorry) and that he gives us a completely new life.

- Tell them about the early Church, how they celebrated this meal and what a wonderful time they had doing it because Jesus was alive and they were living together, loving Jesus and each other in the way that he had shown them and in the way that he had made possible because he had died.
- Tell them about the meal that he has asked us to continue having to remember him; that it is a time when we can be happy and grateful for what he has done for us. Explain about the wine reminding us of Jesus' blood and the bread of his body which was so hurt for us so that we can live as sons and daughters of the King of kings. Also say that we are going to have a wonderful party with Jesus one day and that is something to be excited about.

These points do not have to be related all at one time! They can be communicated through seeing the stories on video, through books, through the Bible, through personal narrative, by acting them out with your children, through drawing and in many other creative ways.

It is important to keep going back to these elements both for us and for our children.

Above all, the children need to know that he did this for them, for your family, and that he lives today and is present when we have this wonderful time together!

Chapter 5

Celebrating communion today

How can we celebrate communion today?

There are many occasions when we can celebrate communion, even daily!

Taking part together in the large group setting has become a time of solemn personal repentance, which can be restored to a time of celebration and a glorious demonstration of the corporate unity of the life of Christ among us. Even changing the music to that of upbeat praise will immediately lift people into a different realm.

Within the corporate setting, families, friends and small groups can take part together, expressing relational love that Jesus died for us to experience. Even as smiles and relational interaction take place, so the meaning of 'celebrating communion' will begin to be expressed.

Whole church meals can also be an expression of communion and corporately reflect the Passover and early Church model seen in the homes.

On the smaller scale there is the interaction and environment of the homes, so clearly seen in biblical times. This could be in the small groups of the church and in the lives of families.

The meal today

Throughout it is important to remember in whose honour the table is prepared and who is the honoured guest at the meal – the Lord Jesus Christ. It is his meal; he is the host and the focus of everyone's attention in the preparation and throughout the whole meal. Jesus is the Incarnate One, present in and through us. Jesus is present to enjoy his people and for his people to enjoy his presence through and with each other.

So even the preparation of the meal in homes, with an atmosphere of joy and celebration, will automatically include the children. The festive atmosphere can be reflected in the choice of food and drink with the bread and wine, or juice, at the central place, so remembering the body and the blood of the sacrificed lamb (Lamb), the now risen King.

Everyone (adults, young people and children) is welcome to the meal. Their personal responsibility is to ensure that they are in unity with everyone present. The meal table so easily exposes friction and discord, but it also exposes joy and true love between those present. The living Body of Jesus at this meal is to reflect the life that Jesus died to give us. Parents need to ensure that their children learn this basic principle and come with welcoming and glad hearts to see their friends and relatives in this setting. The truth is that they are so often quicker to forgive and love than we are! So the meal is taken in a spirit of unity, sincerity, thankfulness and awe, a shared experience, a living testimony of God's people expressing the Gospel.

When everyone is seated the bread can be broken and passed around giving thanks to the Lamb for his body broken and new life of freedom given. This bread was not a small piece but enough to be eaten throughout the meal.

Throughout the meal the atmosphere can be one of a mealtime interaction with questions and answers, from adults and children alike. The conversation centres on the Lamb (the risen Lord) and the impact that he has had on their lives together. It is about personal testimony and explanation.

Creative ways of introducing conversational topics

A decorated box (which a child could make) could be placed in the centre of the table. Inside are pieces of paper that different people (including the children) can pick out at various points during the meal. These could say:

- Ask two people (one could be a child) how they came to know Jesus. This is recounting their experience at the cross/altar.

- Ask each person around the table to say one thing that has made them glad that they are following Jesus. This is expressing the joy of life in the kingdom.
- Ask each person to say something they appreciate about the person sitting on their left. This is the Body being Jesus to each other.

Before the meal ask each person to bring something that expresses or symbolises their new life with Jesus – for example, a flower, symbolising the beauty of Jesus to them; a family picture, symbolising the love between each other that Jesus has given us; a special gift, symbolising the most precious gift of all – Jesus. A special table could be set up, or a central place made for these with the wine and the bread among them as a focus of thanksgiving and praise. At various points during the meal people can explain why they brought their symbol.

Play some quiet praise music quietly in the background. At some point ask people what spoke to them from the music and why it was important to them.

Give each person a quality card and envelope before the meal and ask them to write a love letter to Jesus. At some point during the meal each person reads his or her letter.

One person has a pen and paper during the meal. At various times during the meal ask different people to give one line to create a corporate psalm or lyric. It could be very simple with each person just completing the line 'I love you, Jesus, because . . .' At the time of drinking the wine the whole piece could be read as a corporate offering to Jesus.

The children telling one part of the Passover story could give a short drama.

There are many creative ways in which Jesus can be given the focus. He is a creative God and loves to see us express ourselves through creativity.

At every meal celebrated as communion we are to remind our children why we do this. 'On that day tell your sons, I do this because of what the Lord did for me when He bought me out of bondage' (Exodus 13:8). So we remind our children of the freedom that Jesus' sacrifice has given us. Where today do children get the opportunity to hear regularly the stories that their parents and others have, to hear how God delivered them, to hear of their daily walk in the Kingdom? When do parents hear their children recount their salvation story, their daily walk in the Kingdom? This meal is for everyone to share 'what the Lord did for me when he bought me out of bondage'.

Communion is about a personal testimony of deliverance by the mighty hand of God, never to be forgotten, always remembered through this regular celebration in their homes with their family and maybe relatives and friends. Children love celebrations and this relational natural time will imprint their lives for ever.

Those present have the opportunity to look forward to the celebration in the Father's house where the most lavish banquet will be prepared for us in joy and celebration at the marriage of the Lamb. With excitement and privilege, those at the meal (adults, young people and children) can wonder and imagine what that will be like.

At the end of the meal the wine/juice can be served and drunk – enough for all in plenty. It is a moment to remember, with thanksgiving, the shed blood of the risen Lamb and all that the blood through covenant makes available to us. Understanding covenant is progressive for all of us, and the children will grow in understanding just as we do. The best way for children to understand is through hearing their parents' story and the story of others, by recounting their own testimony, experiencing the meal and corporate celebration, and by being part of a regular celebration where Jesus is the most honoured guest.

Celebrate together

Take the above elements into your culture and your homes, and enjoy with your children the presence of the Lamb of God whose sacrifice today has bought you and your family freedom. Enjoy too the opportunity to celebrate communion in a way that can be a shadow of that glorious time we will share with our children in the Father's house at the wedding feast of the Lamb.

Jesus commanded that we eat together at the meal 'in remembrance of me' (1 Corinthians 11:25). We do this as a reminder for those taking part, adults and children and for the generations to come. Festivals and celebrations are carried on through the generations. Birthdays, Christmas, Thanksgiving are all continued from generation to generation. Jesus commanded us to continue to remember him in this way, to continue to tell our own story of deliverance so that it would be a lasting memorial for the generations to come. Our children will celebrate with their children and their children with future generations.

For the children these times will be indelibly imprinted on their lives. Jesus said that the kingdom belongs to them (Luke 18:16). The meal is of the Kingdom and a visible expression of it. The meal is the time where they can experience the life expressed in their homes and community as revealed in his Body.

Jesus knew best how to pass on remembrance of himself, he wished to be remembered in joyful celebration. Let's do it his way and celebrate communion in our homes with glad and sincere hearts.

Chapter 6
Our love song!

Here is a glimpse into a celebration where the following letter from Jesus was read. Adults and children were then given the opportunity to respond and write their own letter to Jesus. I believe these letters catch the heart of this special celebration.

Jesus' letter:

> Dear ……. (Put your name here)
>
> I'd like you to share my meal! Your birthday is a special time when people remember you. This meal is a special time to remember me. The night before I died for you, I had a meal with my special friends. I told them to remember me by sharing a meal. Every time they ate it they would remember that I died for them.
>
> Now that you are part of my family I want you to remember that I died especially for you. Eat this meal and share it with your friends and family. I will be there too.
>
> You did not do anything to make me love you this much. I just loved you.
>
> As you eat remember that because I died you have a new life.
>
> I love you. I loved you yesterday and I will love you tomorrow. Nothing you can do will change my love for you.
>
> I love you very much.
>
> Jesus

The children's response to Jesus:

> 'Thank you for your letter, I liked it very much. I like you very, very much. With lots and lots and lots of love. Hannah.'
>
> 'Of course I'll come to your meal. I will always love you, I love you like anything. Love from Grace.'
>
> 'Thank you for asking me to your meal. I love you so, so much and will always be your friend. I love you. Tiffany.'
>
> 'You are the bestest friend that anyone could ever have. Love, Kevin.'
>
> 'Thank you very much, Jesus, for your meal. I remember you now, please remember that I love you. I will always try to do what you tell me. All my love, David.'
>
> 'Thank you for your letter. I liked it a lot but I love you more than a letter. You are the best. Love, David.'
>
> 'I love you, Jesus. Thank you for loving me.'
>
> 'Thank you for dying for me. Thank you for loving when you died on the cross. Help me to be a good girl.'
>
> 'Thank you, Jesus, for your love and for being my best friend'
>
> 'Thank you, Jesus, for your love. From Chloe.'

And responses from some of the adults:

> 'Well, Lord, I'm amazed and really I have got to admit that I am very touched by what I heard. I wish I could have known you at such a young age as they are and how much I would have given to have what they have been given. It would have been amazing. So thank you, Lord, for giving it to them.'
>
> 'Thank you, Lord, that we are all your children.'
>
> 'I want to remember you every day; I want to be your best friend too. I love you and my heart goes out when we are together. I want my friendship to grow and I want you to have access to my heart more and more. I want our love to grow like flowers in a garden are growing and I want to hear the bird song in my heart that comes straight from you.'

MISSION STATEMENT

Reconnecting the generations and releasing young people and children to have an uncompromising passion for Jesus with a heart for mission and evangelism

Daphne Kirk is available for conferences, consultations, preaching, teaching and resourcing

Daphne travels internationally working with churches, denominations, missions, church planting initiatives and organisations, so that we can raise a generation that 'loves their God'

(Judges 2:10)

Contact Daphne at
Generation to Generation
E-mail: g2gbusiness@hotmail.com
Tel: +44 (0) 1353 862924

Other books by Daphne Kirk

Hand in hand

Heirs together

Intergenerational cell resources

Let's grow

Reconnecting the generations

What shall we do with the children? (Trainers' manual)

What shall we do with the children? (Trainees' manual)

When a child asks to be baptised

all published by Kevin Mayhew and available from:

KEVIN MAYHEW LTD
Buxhall, Stowmarket, Suffolk, IP14 3BW
E-mail: info@kevinmayhewltd.com

KINGSGATE PUBLISHING INC
1000 Pannell Street, Suite G, Columbia, MO 65201
E-mail: sales@kingsgatepublishing.com